A JOURNEY TO THE CENTRE
OF ONE WOMAN'S HEART

Marianne Brady

BALBOA.
PRESS

A DIVISION OF HAY HOUSE

Balboa Press books may be ordered through booksellers or by contacting:

Balboa Press
A Division of Hay House
1663 Liberty Drive
Bloomington, IN 47403
www.balboapress.com
1-(877) 407-4847

Because of the dynamic nature of the Internet, any Web addresses or links contained in this book may have changed since publication and may no longer be valid. The views expressed in this work are solely those of the author and do not necessarily reflect the views of the publisher, and the publisher hereby disclaims any responsibility for them.

The author of this book does not dispense medical advice or prescribe the use of any technique as a form of treatment for physical, emotional, or medical problems without the advice of a physician, either directly or indirectly. The intent of the author is only to offer information of a general nature to help you in your quest for emotional and spiritual well-being. In the event you use any of the information in this book for yourself, which is your constitutional right, the author and the publisher assume no responsibility for your actions.

Any people depicted in stock imagery provided by Thinkstock are models, and such images are being used for illustrative purposes only.
Certain stock imagery © Thinkstock.

ISBN: 978-1-4525-3228-8 (sc)
ISBN: 978-1-4525-3229-5 (e)

Printed in the United States of America

Balboa Press rev. date: 3/19/2012

CONTENTS

The Beginning..1

Growing Pains..17

Opportunities to Love...27

The Road Ahead...43

Join the Hay Movement...59

From Little Things Big Things Grow.....................69

Home Sweet Home...71

Miracles are Everywhere...77

Believe in Miracles 81

Eyes Wide Open 87

Where Do I Go From Here? 91

THE BEGINNING

Reaching forty was a turning point in my life. Most people say "life begins at forty" and some say "your body takes a turn for the worse" for me it felt like an initiation. I had forty years of my life that I needed to seriously reflect on.

At the age of thirty- three, I began my "spiritual awakening". A Universal Law "when the student is ready the teacher appears" and our teachers are many.

I was standing at the crossroads, wondering which path to take when the universe pointed me in the right direction. It introduced me to a new circle of friends. These friends opened my mind to meditation, astrology, numerology and spirituality and we would often have long discussions about the latest books we were reading. All of this got me hook, line and sinker and I became hungry for knowledge.

The student was ready. It was like a direct link to the Discovery Channel in my head and I didn't know how to turn it off. I wanted to know. Who am I? Why am I here? What is my role in the big scheme of things? I began to read many different kinds of spiritual books. I was like a child in a candy store ready to sample all the delights. I had forgotten how much I loved to read as a child and reading brought back memories of my younger days, although back then I read books to escape from the world.

One of my friends Janelle decided to move back to the Brisbane area and even though we were not very close she told me before she left that she had a feeling that some day we would meet again and become good friends.

"That's nice of her to say that", I thought. But I knew that in my life friends rarely stayed around. We did keep in touch over the phone every now and then. Janelle settled into her new life and was telling me about a new book she had been reading by Louise Hay *The Power Is Within You*. She explained that it had inspired her to enrol in a massage course, something that she had wanted to do for a long time. As her life was changing mine was at a standstill. We lived in a small mining town in central Queensland and even though it was a friendly place, there was not much for women to do while the men were at work.

I was given an invitation to attend a morning tea, a bit like a meet and greet, to get to know the other women in the town. The host was a lovely woman who had her elderly mother staying with her at the time. She went on to tell us that her mother was a psychic who used a deck of playing cards as opposed to tarot cards. We were told she would be available after morning tea if anyone would like a reading. I put my hand up as I had always been fascinated with psychic readings.

During the reading I laughed when she told me that I had a child waiting to be born. This child was very eager and very persistent about being born.

"I don't think so" I said. "I already have three children and I've had my tubes stapled after my last daughter was born, so I am not planning on having any more children".

"Make no mistake this child will do everything in his power to be here. You will recognise him because he will have the most beautiful head of red hair. Never underestimate the power of a soul" she said. Her words echoed in my mind. I went home and told my husband. I can't tell you the exact words he said, but let's just say, he was not a believer!

Months passed and I forgot about the reading until I started having thoughts and urges to have another baby. At this time my third child was just about to start school and my friends thought I was a lunatic.

"Why would you want a baby now, when your youngest is about to start school?" they all said. I know it seemed crazy but I could not get the thought out of my mind. Whoever this soul was it was putting up a good fight, just as the psychic had predicted. When my husband came home from work one day, I asked him how he felt about trying for another baby. He gave me one of his smiles,

"No wonder you only had staples put in those tubes of yours" he said. "There seems to be a pattern. Whenever one of the kids starts school you end up pregnant again. But you do know how much I love making babies?"

"Does that mean you are saying yes?" I asked.

He put his arms around me and gave me a huge hug 'When do we start?' he said.

Before we got our hopes up however I made an appointment with a gynaecologist to find out about tubal reversal. The doctor told us our chances for a positive outcome were 99%, due to my tubes having been stapled not tied. He believed the staples could be removed without causing any damage to my tubes.

"The operation will involve a large incision, much the same as a C- section, so it is not without risks. Go home and discuss it and call me if you have any concerns" the doctor said. This child was not going to leave me alone, so I agreed to the operation. Recovery was quite painful but the procedure was a complete success. Within three months I was pregnant. Our beautiful red haired boy was born September 1993. The psychic was right!

My belief in a higher power was helped by the birth of my son.

Maybe this was the actual beginning of my awakening?

When my son was one year old, we moved to another mining town. That's when I received a phone call from my friend Janelle to see how we were settling in.

"Guess what" she said " we are moving back up there to live and the boys [husbands] will be working together again, just like old times". That was the best news that I had heard in a while. I was struggling to make new friends and Janelle and I had had some lengthy conversations over the phone. I had never forgotten her comment about the two of us meeting again and becoming good friends.

Janelle was going through an exciting stage of growth in her life and to be around her was inspiring. She was now a qualified massage therapist and she had a passion for vitamins and natural therapies. She had also decided to open a Health Food Store and massage clinic in town. This made sense as the only vitamins you could buy were either from the supermarket, through the mail or you made a trip into the larger city three hundred kilometres away. Janelle asked if I would like to become her assistant due to the fact that when we first met I had sparked her interest in vitamins. My knowledge of vitamins came from my mother whom I called the "vitamin queen".

It was an exciting time for both of us. I had always wanted to work in the health industry and Janelle was a most amazing and inspiring businesswoman. My life became very

hectic. I had two jobs as well as being a very busy mother. I worked at a supermarket filling shelves at night and then I would work at the Health food store through the day.

I was in awe of Janelle. She was smart and very sure of herself. She became my mentor.

I always loved being at the shop. It opened up a whole new world for me. I soon became interested in massage and wanted to learn, but I had very low self esteem.

One day I asked Janelle, "How do you do it? How did you become so confident?".

She showed me the book *The Power Is within You* by Louise Hay.

"Remember how I told you this book changed my life and gave me the courage to follow my passion? Now it is time for you to do the same and to follow your passion" she said.

I wasn't completely convinced but I took the book home anyway.

The book gave me the tools to discover my own hidden strengths. It also discussed the power behind the spoken word. The book explained how to change, how to reprogram the way you think and how to believe in yourself. I did the exercises and started to say the daily affirmations as described in the book. I wasn't sure if it was going to work but I was willing to try. I compiled my own small list of affirmations to start with and placed them on my bathroom mirror, on the fridge and even in my purse. These were:

"I follow my own intuition of what feels right for me".

"I am a free spirit who knows how to love her-self and others".

"I can relate to people in a more loving, compassionate way".

"I give out love and joy and find it where ever I turn".

"I believe I am wonderful and life is a joy".

"I love and approve of myself and easily make changes".

I repeated the affirmations daily until they became second nature to me.

(All affirmations adapted from The Power Is Within You) Louise. L. Hay.

A couple of weeks later the local paper advertised a massage course. "What perfect timing I thought" It was now or never so I picked up the phone and enrolled.

D-day arrived and I was very nervous. It brought back memories of my school days. This time the uniform had to be your underwear and not a school uniform. I was not comfortable getting undressed in front of strangers. Then I thought we are all in the same boat so just get on with it! Old familiar thoughts came creeping in "What are you doing here? You can't do this! You're going to fail as usual". I closed my eyes took a deep breath and just kept repeating these words to myself,

"YOU CAN DO THIS. Don't listen to your ego, listen with your heart".

To my amazement I passed the course and topped the class with 98%. My confidence soared to a new level. I was so proud of myself. Whenever I became nervous I silently would ask my Angels and guides for their help and they would come through loud and clear. I felt that I could do anything. The next phase in my life had begun. I quickly became a workshop junkie. I studied Kinesiology, Reiki, Crystal Healing and many more alternative therapies. I was searching for something that felt like me but I didn't really know what that something was. The real journey started when I realized that I was not my past and that I needed to 'let go and forgive'. I am not quite sure how I got there, only that it felt like I was travelling in a parallel universe.

I next decided to participate in a re -birthing workshop facilitated by a Catholic Nun. It was a small group and I had no idea what to expect. I thought it involved meditation and visualisation. Boy, was I wrong! I watched some of the other participants go through the re-birthing process. My first thought was "What the hell have I signed up for?" It reminded me of the movie *One Flew OverThe Cuckoo's Nest* starring Jack Nicholson.

The other participants in the workshop were wailing, screaming and rolling around on the floor. I wanted to run and I started scanning for the closest exit.

When I heard a soothing and gentle voice inside my head say "Ok Marianne you can do this".

It was the most profound thing lying there in a foetal position and seeing myself for the first time as a tiny baby. I was witnessing my entry into the world. I felt cold, rejected and I was not happy at being forced out of the womb where I had felt safe and protected.

I was already feeling fear and my life had only just begun. A deep spiritual wound of feeling disconnected from something, but what? The re-birthing process inspired me to start writing poetry again. A pattern was beginning to emerge, every time I felt disconnected in my life, a growth spurt would follow.

Writing became a wonderful discovery tool for me and I urge everyone to make it a part of their journey. The following poem I wrote after the re-birthing workshop.

The Time Has Come

The time had come to reflect upon, my childhood years,
To find the reason for the tears,
Sometimes tears of joy, sometimes tears of sadness.
Life would have been easier if I was a boy,
It would have put an end to all of my madness.
As I reached my teenage years, I brought with me all my childhood fears.
How could I be sure where I belonged, when did my life start going horribly wrong.
I was feeling ashamed and believed that I was to blame,
I didn't want anyone to know my name.
Please Lord I cried, why do I want to run and hide?
Nobody knew how I felt deep inside, I was certain, there was no one there by my side,
Who chose this life for me?
Who is it that I am supposed to be?
Please dear God set me free

I began to keep a daily journal jotting down insights that came to me throughout the day and from my meditations. I continued to search for more books on self-help, meditation, and spiritual healing. I then decided to read Louise Hays bestselling book *"You Can Heal Your Life"*. I began to again recite affirmations. I knew this time I needed to work on forgiving the past. After reading Louise's life story I felt my life was in parallel with her story.

Mary Heath, a *Heal Your Life* teacher came to our area and I attended my first '*Heal Your Life Workshop*'. Mary was the only teacher in Australia at that time. The workshop was exhausting and it brought up a lot of old hurts. Finally I was able to heal. I felt lighter somehow for the first time in my life.

I worked hard to become a better person and to understand the process. I remember thinking one day I am going to teach this.

My new affirmations were about forgiveness and acceptance.

"The door of my heart is wide open and I am safe to love".
"I am a powerful channel for the healing power of love".
"I am willing to experience all the joys of life, life loves me and I am safe".
"I live in the present moment and I easily release all past pain".

Janelle's massage clinic was getting busier. It soon became clear that the responsibility for the Health Food shop as well as the massage was proving to be too much, especially with the shop opening seven days a week.

Janelle loved the shop but she knew it was time for her to sell and to concentrate on her massage career. The shop was on the market for a little while but no serious buyer's came forward. It was a hard time in the town financially and Janelle was tossing up with the idea of just closing the doors and cutting her losses .As the shop was like my second home and I did not want it to close Janelle came up with the idea to sell the shop to me. "Me a shop owner? But I know nothing about business" I thought. But Janelle had planted the seed! I went home and talked it over with my husband who by now was used to my way-out ideas. I pleaded with him to think about it, "I really, really want this". I explained. Like a child pestering a parent. We agreed to go to the bank together to see what our chances were. Luckily for us the bank allowed us to take out a personal loan. I became the proud owner of a Health Food business. I kept pinching myself to see if it was real or if it was a dream.

How did I get to here? All my dreams were coming true. Me, the girl who hadn't finished school. I had no formal business training only that which Janelle passed on to me. "If I can do it" she said "then so can you". I was so glad that she believed in me. My parents were also very proud and happy that their little girl was finally doing something with her life! I was also beginning to believe in me too.

This is the first step in changing your life, challenging all the old beliefs of who you thought you were and creating new belief patterns of who you would like to become.

It was tough on my family. They had to adjust not only to me being at the shop seven days a week but to also adapt to my new beliefs about life. Every mother wants the best for her family and like any new spiritual seeker you feel you want your family to share in those beliefs. This was before I knew that you can't change anybody else, you can only change yourself. (Another Universal Law). I think the children felt abandoned by me and they were growing up fast. I also felt it was time for them to gain some independence.

The shop to me was my new baby. I needed it as much as it needed me. I had had a childhood dream of owning and running a healing centre and the shop was fulfilling that dream. It took all my energy, and when I got home, I didn't have anything left to give my family. I was meeting many new people and forging new friendships, something that I never had while growing up. I really began to feel very blessed. Pauline was the shops resident Tarot reader. She always filled the shop with laughter and she was a loving and caring counsellor to so many people, including me. My friend Bronwyn introduced me to Auric healing and spirit guides. She also held meditation groups and workshops. She has since proven to be a wonderful healing presence for the planet. Over the years many different therapists and healers worked from the shop and helped to make it into a healing haven.

It was never a profitable business but it was a network centre for like minded people to gather and it became known among all my friends as the 'Lighthouse'. I started a very popular lending library with all the books I had gathered over the years. It gave me a sense of giving back to the community. I was grateful to help so many people and to see their lives change. I began to see a different side of me that I had hidden for years. My walls and barriers were starting to crumble. I was learning a lot about me and my beliefs were being challenged on a daily basis and little did I know there was a lot more to come.

Ever wonder what happens when you open a huge can of worms? It is not easy to keep track of them all. I saw a different side of myself, one that I had not seen since I was little. I was having trouble convincing myself that I was a worthy person. I was carrying lots of baggage, self-hate, guilt and I felt like a fake. People were saying loving things to me because I had helped them. But I worried if they *really* knew me would they would still love me? My past was haunting me because I had done many things in my younger days that I was not proud of, I did not feel deserving of anyone's love. Wayne Dyer (Inspirational Hay House author) wrote the acronym for ego as *Edging God Out*. My ego was doing its best to do just that, keeping God out of my life.

I was able to be a bubbly, warm hearted and friendly person at the shop. That was who I longed to be but underneath I was far from that type of person. My children saw a very different side of me. When I came home it was all about discipline and housework. I was an angry tired mum and the last thing I wanted to do when I came home was housework. I would constantly yell because the house was untidy, by my standards, not to theirs. They were messy and I criticized them constantly. They probably felt they could do nothing right. I had expectations of how the house should look and I expected the children to know that. Where did that belief come from? From my parents of course!. I am not saying my parents were wrong. I know they did the best they could with the knowledge they had as it was passed on to them by their parents. It was then passed on to me. I had too many expectations of how everything should be, instead of just being satisfied with the way things were. So my new affirmation became: *"not perfect but good enough"*.

It certainly did not help that my brain's programme was hard wired, to expect a messy house, so when I arrived home from work, there it was, a self- fulfilling prophecy.

I wanted to be different around my children. I loved them, but I was unsure how to show it. I now realize it was my own feelings of unworthiness. I never felt like a good mother and they were so beautiful. I always wondered why God had put them in my care.

It has been said that our children choose us and not the other way round. This is for the purpose of their life lessons. We as parents are just playing our role in the movie of their lives. We each have our scripts and it is how we deliver the lines that will determine the outcome. The trick is to know when you are a part of the script and when you are the spectator. It is so easy to get caught up in someone else's drama. My role in the game of life I hope will be a memorable one. So next time your teenagers are giving you a hard time, remember that they chose you.

Why?

Why is the sky blue and the earth so brown?
Why must I sit here and always frown?
There is so much for me to learn,
To get away is what I yearn.
To be quiet and still to go within,
Where does it start? Where do I begin?
I long to be the person I am meant to be,
To flow like the river, gentle and free.
So many people now cross my path,
I don't know what to say or what to ask.
How do I know the difference between light and
dark?

GROWING PAINS

I grew up in a middle class family, my father was a coal miner and my mother worked most of her life as a cleaner. I have many memories of my childhood some wonderful and some not so good. All of the memories are woven into the fabric of who I am. When little my world was a fantasy world. I played with fairies in the garden, they were my little secret and my favourite books were Enid Blyton's ***Tales of Toyland*** and ***The Magic Faraway Tree***. I used to dream of having my own hospital for all the animals and toys. I imagined the toys were alive, much like watching a cartoon on television. The outside world was very strange to me, too many rules and regulations and not enough fun! I did not understand society's class system or the rules of a religion. My family was catholic and I struggled with the churches beliefs from an early age. The nuns at the Catholic school I attended seemed cranky and often cruel. The rule 'love thy neighbour as thy self' didn't always apply.

I will never forget going to confession and listening to a nun who told us to "tell the Father your sins and if you don't have any to make them up". That was a defining moment for me. I wondered

"Why would God want me to be naughty?" The response was "In order for God to love you you have to be a sinner".

The world was starting to look and feel like a scary place. Being very shy I did not want to draw attention to myself so I followed the rules and did what I was told to do. I can now see that fear kept us caught up in old patterns of religious dogma and we accepted that as Truth. This I believe goes against everything that God stands for.

I felt like a captured animal up until I turned fifteen. That is when I told my parents I was not going back to church. School however was even worse for me. It was a constant battlefield. You either became tough quickly or you were picked on. Such it seemed was the law of nature. I was a bit of a tomboy as I grew up with my only brother Stephen, two years my senior. We were best mates. I enjoyed being around the boys, playing beach cricket and building cubby houses in the bush. My early years were spent growing up near a lake. It was a beautiful place. My brother and I used to love swimming in the lake when it was raining, our mother didn't understand, she thought we were crazy. All the neighbours were like family. My parents got on really well with a couple who had two boys the same age as my brother and I and they lived next door. There were many kids in our neighbourhood and my memories of these early times are happy ones.

One Christmas the boys next door got a tennis table. We would all play together most every day after school and on the weekends. We became quite good at the game and then their father suggested we start a club. We approached the local hall and set up a night for enrolments. The club became very popular and soon our family was involved in the committee along with the next door neighbours' father. We would still practice in the neighbours' garage every day after school. One afternoon while the boys were playing their father asked me to come up stairs as he wanted to show me something special for the club. He asked me to follow him into his bedroom and as I trusted him completely I did as I was told. This man was like a second father to me. He then told me to sit on the bed and to close my eyes as there was going to be a surprise for me. I was only ten years old at the time. What ten year olds didn't like surprises? He then asked me to hold out my hand which I did. Whatever it was it felt very unfamiliar. He held his hand over mine and began to make jerking movements still telling me to keep my eyes closed. I began to feel frightened, something was not right! I opened my eyes. I screamed when I saw I was holding his penis. He put his hand over my mouth before I could scream again and began to tell me how much he loved me. He then explained "This is what people do when they love each other. It's really ok, this can be our little secret", he said. Then he said that if I would stay he would buy me lots of presents. I pushed him away and ran out of the house down to my favourite spot on the lake. I was so scared. I wondered why he would do something like that to me. Was there something wrong with me? I didn't understand. I stayed there until it got dark and it felt safe to go home. I did not want to tell my parents because he was their friend. I felt that I had done something terrible and I feared they would not believe me. All I could think about was being punished if anyone were to find out.

After this I kept to myself and I would only go to the garage with my brother when I knew the boy's father was not home. I quit the table tennis club and told my parents I was sick of it. They thought I was having another tantrum. Even though nothing else happened after that day, I had changed. I felt the sweet young girl that loved life was gone. Life as I knew it seemed no longer to love me. That day changed my view of the world. A war had broken out in my heart and an inner battle had started within me. On the outside I began a battle with the people around me. I believed that people who wanted to get close were doing it for one reason, to hurt me. My parents decided to send me to a Catholic girl's high school. I hated it, the girls talked about boys constantly and I had to ride on the train home for an hour every day with all the Catholic boys. The boys saw me as a challenge as I appeared to be a tough girl. I was a confused and angry teenager who thought in order to get love you had to hurt someone. Of course I attracted all the wrong boys, rebels without a cause. I would skip school and spend my days at the beach. My parents became disheartened with me. They didn't understand why I acted this way and I certainly didn't want to listen to what they had to say. As a last resort my parents attempted to send me to a counsellor. Their picture of who their little girl should be didn't fit and our arguments became worse. I wanted their life to be miserable, just like mine. They were trying to give me a better life than the one they had experienced growing up.

I now know that as a parent we try to cushion our children from pain and that was what my parents were trying to do for me. As parents we want what we think is best for our children however in order for them to grow they need to face life's tests. We assume we know what is right for them and to quote my husband 'you know what happens when you ass-u-me? You make an ass out of you and me." I loved my parents dearly and I know they had great expectations of me, only I could not be who they wanted me to be.

I now know the battle was never with my parents, it was within me. You can only find out what is right or wrong for you if you follow your heart and overstep the boundaries. I believed I was a failure in my parent's eyes and in society's eyes as well.

I decided to quit school and I started work at the local supermarket. I was fourteen years and nine months, just the legal age to get a job. It felt good to be independent. For the first time in my life I had my own money and I hoped maybe my parents would let go of the reigns and give me more freedom.

I started a relationship with a boy who was also angry at the world and with his parents. Now I know he was a reflection of me and my life at that time. He had dropped out of school but he wasn't working. We were like two peas in a pod and we thought we had it all figured out. Him and me against the world! He introduced me to marijuana and we would lose ourselves in our make believe world. The drugs and alcohol started to make him paranoid accusing me of absurd things. Over time he became increasingly violent and verbally abusive and then he would beg for my forgiveness. And as always I believed him and welcomed him back. Just when I thought my life could not get any worse, I found out I was pregnant. I was sixteen and about to become a mum. I was terrified and not sure how I was going to break the news to my parents. They did not approve of my boy friend, so how would they react when I was to tell them I am about to have his baby?

My father cried. I could see the disappointment and shame in his eyes.

"Look at what you have done with your life you have ruined it. You will never amount to anything", he said. My mother was angry and wanted to know how I was going to look after the baby, when I was still a child myself. I had made up my mind this was my baby and I was going to show everyone that I could be a good mother.

It was hard for me to adjust to the criticisms of society. I felt I had become a social outcast. Even my friends did not want to hang out with me anymore as I was a bad influence. I was terrified of giving birth so the doctor sent me along with my mother to watch a birthing video at the hospital. Just at the end when the baby was about to come out of the birth canal, my mother passed out on the floor.

"Oh great" I thought "is she going to do that when it's my turn?" She was my only support person and she couldn't watch a baby being born!. The labour was a difficult one, traumatic for the baby and me. My darling mother would you believe was wonderful under pressure. During my labour the nurses were unable to find my doctor so I had the locum on duty. I didn't blame my baby for not wanting to be born. I knew how he felt, the world was a pretty harsh place to be and I was going to be his mother!

After my son was born I moved in with the baby's father at his parent's place and so we became a real family. My son's father loved and adored his son but the responsibility of looking after us was too much for him. He struggled to find a job and when he did find one he had trouble keeping it. Soon he became more distant. He would spend all day drinking and smoking with his mates and I knew he was seeing other girls.

Then one day, while visiting my parents, our son became upset and I couldn't pacify him. My partner started yelling at me to "shut the baby up". I yelled back and he took a swipe at my head and missed hitting the baby instead. An argument then broke out between my partner and my brother and they both ended up in hospital. When visiting my partner he started complaining about my family and how everything was their fault. He didn't want anything more to do with them and he told me that I had to choose between him and my family. I took the baby and went for a walk. I thought long and hard trying to envision the future for me, and my son. Did I really want to stay in this relationship? I went back to the room, looked my partner in the eye and told him my decision. "I choose my family. You lose" I said. He screamed at me and told me to get out of the room. He then warned me that he would make my life a living hell. "What" I yelled back. "You think that my life isn't already a living hell". I vowed that day that I deserved a better life and so did my son.

Looking back at my life I now realise how strong I was. Don't get me wrong I was afraid. Afraid of being a single parent wondering if any anybody else could love me because I was damaged goods! My partner continued to harass me. He constantly stalked me and made threatening phone calls. I became a nervous wreck. I decided to talk with his parents to see if they could talk some sense into him. I didn't want him to miss out on his son, but he was like a loose cannon and I couldn't allow him access until he calmed down. They did speak with him and convinced him to be more rational. This then allowed him to visit. This was hard for me as I knew I still had feelings for him.

Then one day I made the mistake of sleeping with him and soon discovered I had again fallen pregnant. My son was only three months old. How stupid was I to have put myself in this situation. I told my mother and my best friend that I could not go through with this pregnancy. They arranged for me to get help at a local clinic for young girls. My friend drove me to the appointment. It was terrible but I felt I had no choice. I could not go through with having another child to this man and to be forced to stay in the relationship. I had to be honest with him that this was the end. He agreed but he also explained how hard it was for him to see his son for just short visits. He felt that because he could not be there for his son all the time the best thing he could do for us was to let us go. "I want my son to have a real family. Not a dysfunctional one" he said. We then parted and I was a single mum.

I was now stronger and I was gaining a new outlook on life. I was ready for a new beginning. That's when my knight in shining armour arrived. He loved my son and me! Even though I was standing at the crossroads once again I knew I had now chosen the right path.

I married the love of my life in October 1980 and thirty years on we are still together. The growing pains have been many but they have made me and my husband stronger and ready to face what god has in store for us, on this magical mystery tour.

I believe fate brought us together. I met my husband at my best friend's wedding, a month before I had separated from my ex. He was the best man and I was maid of honour, we sat and talked all night. There was an amazing connection between us. I felt safe in his presence. I did not want that day to end to go back to face my other life. When he took me home he said "if you ever decide to leave that boyfriend of yours I'll be waiting". The stage was set and a month later I left my boyfriend and my knight was waiting for me. Just as he said he would be.

Our real journey had now begun the past was setting us up for the future, so we buckled our seatbelts and hung on feeling a little fearful of the road ahead.

Relationships

In the stillness, I hope you find what you are
looking for,
In the darkness, I hope your fears are conquered.
In the light, I hope your friendships will be forged,
In your heart, I hope you will find its beauty.
Plant your seeds of love for tomorrow,
Some will perish and cause you sorrow,
Some will go on to grow and bloom,
But leave behind their sweet perfume.
Where they end up, only you will know,
For only you can choose the way,
Some will leave and some will stay,
Blessed are all who will cross your path,
For they are your biggest teachers,
Hold their memories only in your heart,
Knowing they lovingly played their part.

OPPORTUNITIES TO LOVE

*R*eviewing my life I now realise I carried all the baggage from my past into the future. Hate, resentment, blame and guilt. But I also found that the universe always manages to bring you the people and the opportunities to heal if you are ready. I had asked God to show me who I was. Little did I know that you have to find out who you aren't, before you can find out who you truly are. Looking back I realise it's like finding the pieces to a jigsaw puzzle. The more you struggle to find the pieces the more lost you become. Then bingo the next piece jumps out at you.

The next piece of the puzzle came when a friend gave me a DVD to watch and I cannot recall the title or who was in it. My friend did not know much about me and my life at this point she just thought it was a great movie and thought I might like to watch it before it had to go back to the video store.

The movie was all about women who had chosen or who were forced into having abortions for different reasons in their lives. I settled on the sofa, feeling good at being home alone and having some quality time to myself, which was very rare. The movie made me recall the memories of my own abortion, gut wrenching emotions, I couldn't stop the tears. I just let the flood gates open and sobbed my heart out. My husband came home from work and wondered what was wrong when he saw me huddled on the couch like a wounded animal. I had not told him about my abortion, I was too ashamed, only my mother and my friend knew. "What sort of a person will he think I am?" I wondered. I was waiting for his judgement, but none came, he took me in his arms and held me while I cried.

That was when I first began to realise the Soul's Way. That DVD was no accident, I was ready to heal the shame and guilt that I was carrying from the abortion .I was told by the Angels that the souls are not present until just before birth, I believe that every soul has a choice and they choose whether their life experience enhances their learning or not.

I am not saying that abortion is the right thing to do. I am only speaking from my own experience. It felt like the right choice for me at the time and I have accepted that it was all part and parcel of my Souls' Way. It gave me the opportunity to love myself even more.

My journey into the centre of my heart was a long one and many times I felt like giving up. I am grateful for the guidance of my Angels, who always gave me the answers that I needed. The answers came through my writing and poetry. The eyes are the windows to the soul and of our perception of the world. However everyone sees life differently through their own lenses or maybe rose coloured glasses.

The Angels were trying to show me the glass half-full, not the glass half empty. All I could see though were the cracks and they were starting to appear.

The Eyes Have It

Life is never easy I know,
Without these little trials,
None of us would grow,
Into the beautiful beings,
That we are destined to be,
Like the birds in the trees,
The oceans and the seas,
Like the colours of the rainbow,
That we all seek to find,
We are all those colours,
Yet we choose to be blind.
What joy you will have,
When you finally choose to see,
Be all you can be, set yourself free,
The world is waiting for a shining star,
Create your magic, wherever you are.

The shop had run its own course. It had helped many people who had came through its doors or sat on its veranda. In August 2001 I made the heart wrenching decision to close the shop. I had been in the process of selling the shop to my friend Chris, who has now left her earthly existence. She had been involved in the shop from the very beginning. Now that I was ready to move on I had decided that Chris would be the next caretaker. We had drawn up the contracts with my lawyer, so that she could take over the repayments of my loan as she was unable to get a bank loan. Chris was a wonderful therapist and who had the passion that I no longer had. It had reached a point where the shop was taking up my whole life, placing a drain on me physically and mentally. My family and my marriage were beginning to suffer. I felt it was time for me to remain at home and to regain my sanity. I did try to sell the shop on the open market at first, but I had no luck, the town was going through a down-turn and many families had left.

The shop I believe was following it's own divine plan and I had no control over what was to come.

Just when we were ready to sign all the contracts Christine's world took a dive. She was diagnosed with breast cancer. She was scared of conventional medicine and the doctors didn't offer her much hope. Christine then put all her energy into finding a natural alternative. She cleaned her house and discarded every product containing chemicals. She followed a strict routine of daily coffee enemas, raw juices and large doses of vitamin C. Her strong determination and will was remarkable to witness. Everyone who knew her thought she would overcome her disease, she never gave up on finding a cure.

I wanted so much for her to realize her dream, to be the owner of the shop. To pass on the gift that had been given to me, as some would say to "pay it forward". Months had gone by and her condition did not improve. She no longer was well enough to come to the shop. I went to visit her at home and the doctor was administering her medication. She was slipping away from us and yet she still hoped for a miracle, as we all did. This was the first time I had witnessed a person clinging on to life with determination in a body so frail. I went home and cried, knowing that I could not fulfil her dream. I also knew I could not stay at the shop any longer, I was keeping it open for her and the time had come to close it. I will never forget going to her house to tell her that the shop was no longer. Tears streamed down her face. I think in that moment she finally realized that she was dying. She was so upset to find out. At first she had a look of disbelief and then the realisation that others believed that she would not survive. The shop had helped her to keep her faith alive. Now her dream would never be realized. It broke my heart to see the look in her eyes of her dreams and hopes lost. I was also hanging on to a dream that I knew was just that a "dream" and it was time to let the dream go. The shop had become part of my identity so when it closed a part of me died too.

A few days later I went to visit Christine to explain that she was a much loved figure in the community and that her life did serve a purpose. I explained how her passion for massage and natural therapies had helped hundreds of people to restore their health. She sincerely wanted to help people and she had done this many times. I took with me a poem I had written for her. Christine asked me to read to her the poem and at this time she appeared to be in good spirits. During that visit we hugged and cried for what seemed to be a very long time. That was the last time I saw Christine. One week after I closed the shop she passed away on the 8th of September 2001. Her funeral was held on a lovely sunny day and many people turned out to say their goodbyes. At the end of the service at her request we blew bubbles and let them float up to the sky. The bubbles danced in the sunlight as they made their way up to heaven while the songs *"Love Is all Around You"*, *"Many Rivers to Cross"* and *"Amazing Grace"* played. Her wish was granted that her farewell from this world was a celebration of her life.

Angel Friend

My dear sweet angel friend,
I cannot begin to know your pain,
Of unshed tears, for years you carry,
Lifetimes of pain for there were many.
My dear sweet angel friend,
You are a pillar of strength, courage and
determined will,
While amongst the storm, you show a calm centre
still.
I wish you well, my sweet angel friend,
Although your heart may hurt now, I know it will
soon mend.
Many hearts will blossom and open together,
By simply having known you, my sweet angel
friend.

Now that the shop was closed I had my own demons to face. I became racked with pain and guilt. We were in debt for $10,000 dollars for the shop loan. My mind was riddled with doubt and fear. I wondered "What if I had kept the shop open for longer would Chris still be alive?" "What about all the people I have let down? How am I going to fix this mess?" I could not see the forest for the trees.

I found it difficult adjusting to life again, I felt ashamed to go out in public. My husband was busy training for triathlons so we did not see a lot of each other. It felt like we were living separate lives. We used to be each other's best friend but we had forgotten how to communicate. We had become strangers in our own home. He had become accustomed to not having me around and he had a lot of freedom to do what he wanted. Now that I was home every day he began to feel guilty about his training schedule. The children on the other hand were glad to have me home they nearly smothered me. However I wasn't aware of just how dysfunctional as a family we had become. This was highlighted when our eldest daughter told us she was pregnant and to a guy she barely knew. History was repeating itself! She was eighteen and pregnant, about to become a single mum and I was to be a grandma at forty but this event actually brought us closer as a family. My husband, my friend Janelle and I were there for the birth of our first grandchild. It was amazing to witness the actual birth of our granddaughter, my husband cut the cord and I cleaned her up and gave her her first bath. When I was pregnant my husband had always beaten me to the hospital if I was in labour and he was at work. He would tell me how wonderful it was to watch the births but he could never convince me until that moment. It was a truly amazing experience and I felt honoured to be there for this new little soul's entry into the world.

Granddaughter

'Who are you' little girl, I think I recognize that
beautiful face,
You have a purpose for being here, to bring light to
this place.
Your heart is pure and filled with a song,
You will unite the nation bring them home where
they belong.
For love peace and glory, you will rewrite their
story,
To heal the land, of ages past,
We have all been waiting for you here you are at
long last.

Life became busy with a new baby in the house. I had trouble dividing my time amongst everyone and I was feeling hemmed in. I wanted to spend quality time with my husband, time with my children and our baby granddaughter but I also needed some me time.

I was beginning to lose myself in everyday chaos. My spiritual journey began to feel like it was all a dream. My family, I believe, thought it was some crazy faze I was going through but it was real to me and I didn't want to lose what I felt was my purpose to find me. My children said I was weird and my husband would tell people that I howled at the moon! I wondered "could I be a wife, a mother and a spiritual seeker too?" To get time out I decided to go back to work as a housemaid at a local motel. I never thought I would go back to cleaning and I did feel like I was going backwards but I also felt the universe had a plan.

With my return to work my husband brought himself a computer. I however felt this new 'toy' took away our quality time when we were able to get time together. My husband constantly spent time on the computer and emailed his workmates even on his days off.

He accessed a website to find old classmates. Initially I thought it was a good idea not that I wanted to access it myself. My husband would often call me in when he received funny emails or if he got a reply back from an old classmate. He would receive emails from one particular girl. I didn't mind, I trusted him, after all it was just a computer. We had a lot going on in our life finding time for each other became less and less.

My husband started to spend quite a lot more time on the computer. Sometimes he would suggest I go shopping with the girls.

I would come home and find the computer room door shut. This he had never done before and when I walked in, he would change the computer screen. I started to become suspicious, something didn't feel right and I tried to joke about it, saying he must be looking at naked ladies but instead he became agitated and moody. I started to resent the fact that he spent all his spare time on the computer. I felt I needed love and attention too. The more I tried the more he pushed me away. My best friend Janelle became my surrogate partner. She was there for me, when he wasn't. One night while my husband was on nightshift I sat at the computer, I wanted to know what everyone else saw in these machines. I began reading the emails when I came across one from a lady from my husband's school. It explained how much she needed him and loved him. At first I thought it was a joke. Then I discovered more emails, photos and songs they had sent to each other. I could not believe what I was seeing, the blood rushed to my head and I thought I was going to pass out. I sat down on the floor and started to cry. Why was this happening to me? The man I loved, the man I had spent 20 years with was betraying me. When I confronted him he had no answers, it had started out as just "words" he said, it didn't mean anything. She however was saying all the right things that he wanted to hear. He told me that he would delete her emails from the computer and that would be it. But it didn't end there. They continued to talk to each other on the phone when I was out of the house. Each time I caught him talking to her and he would say he wouldn't do it again I actually believed him.

Here I was again living a nightmare. Then my husband told me that the two of them had slept together. They had taken their relationship to another level. I tried to be strong for the children. I did not want them to see me upset, but I had become that ten-year-old girl again, my heart could not take anymore. I blamed myself I thought if I had not gone on a stupid spiritual quest none of this would have happened. I wanted desperately to keep my family together but I was falling apart, the fire in my heart was burning out of control and I didn't know how to extinguish it .

We went to counselling but there was just so much hurt, I could not get past the betrayal. Then he came home and said he didn't love me anymore, it was over. I was devastated. I was trying so hard to be what he wanted, but it was too late. I had failed again. I moved out of the house and into our caravan. My husband helped me move into the local caravan park, for the first two days I cried continuously. I had never felt so alone. Then one night he came to the van and asked me to come home. He explained he was sorry for what he had put me through, he wanted to work it out and he felt the kids missed me. I went home with him believing every word he said. It was only then that I found out he had tricked me into moving back home as he felt guilty about me living in the van instead of him. The next day he moved into the van. I was so angry. How could he play with my feelings this way? He had held me in his arms the night before and then got up the next morning as if nothing had happened. I locked myself in my room with bottles of red wine and started drinking. I started screaming at the top of my lungs smashing the bottles against the walls. My children began screaming outside the door to let them in. They went and rang my friend Janelle who came over to try to coax me out of the room. "I am not coming out until he comes here to talk with me" I screamed. I wanted some answers. My husband came and he was not happy at being summoned and when I looked into his cold steely eyes, I did not see the man I loved nor one who loved me.

I pleaded "Please tell me why this is happening?" Again he had no answers but he told me he had asked the woman to come and live with him and it was finally over. Our life together was over. I did not know why. I had trusted him completely and now he was gone. This was the theme of my life. It was my fault I said to myself. "You've done it again Marianne. You put your trust in someone and you always get hurt". To cope I took an overdose of pills. The next thing I was waking up in hospital. My children had come home and tried to wake me, when I would not move they called the ambulance. I was very depressed when I discovered I was still alive. My husband was there beside my bed when I woke up and all I could think about was that I didn't want him to be there if he was only there out of pity. I wanted everyone to piss off and leave me alone. To leave me to grieve the life that had died. When they allowed me to go home I was under family surveillance. They watched my every move. The doctor prescribed antidepressants and I had to have video conferences with a psychotherapist. When the time came for the doctor to say I was able to return home I thought How is my life better? The man I love still doesn't love me? He was in my life out of duty. Duty to the children and to make sure their mother was okay.

I was angry with God. I felt betrayed by him for leading me into this deep dark hole. I felt this journey had led me into despair and heartache. All roads seemed to lead back to hell. It was like being in a monopoly game and always missing GO. I could not see a clear path ahead. It was even more painful for me to watch my family in pain. Every day was a struggle the darkness had fully engulfed me. I had forgotten how to function, and I was moving around on autopilot. The grief was too much for me to handle and I took another overdose, ending up once again in hospital. My family and friends became hostile toward my husband and blaming him for my problems. I then told them if they acted this way towards him we would never have the opportunity to heal our wounds.

I saw a different side to Suicide through my experience. I truly believed that the world would be a better place without me and I was doing my family and friends a favour by leaving them to live their lives without me because I would only 'stuff things up'. You feel it is too hard to talk to others about how you are feeling. My insights made me believe that no one could help me anyway. When you feel like this you blame yourself for making a mess of everyone's lives. **Families often carry guilt about suicide because they feel they should have seen the signs. I believe society has helped people to hide their feelings and scorned those who let their feelings out. It is a very painful process facing your feelings. You feel like you are in the eye of the tornado that picks you up, tosses you from side to side, bruised and weather-beaten. This can happen very fast. The tornado tossed me out, not once, but twice. Here I was waiting for the dust to settle, so I could see my way clear. God had other plans for me, I tried to search for the light often, but I had grown so accustomed to the dark that I had allowed it to swallow me whole. Forced to sit in the void and wait for the light to coax me out. I knew this feeling well, unworthiness, abandonment and it would keep manifesting in my life until I was able to trust and heal it.**

Weeks went by and my family and I were slowly healing, taking each day as it came. I hated feeling out of control,

desperately still seeking answers. Until one day I sat quietly and asked God "why has this happened to me? The answer that came floored me. "You asked for it child." My response was "you have got to be kidding me! I asked for all this?"

"Remember child when you were so engrossed in your spiritual growth. You told me that you felt you did not belong with your family, that they didn't understand you anymore and that they would probably be better off without you. You also stated you wanted to be free to pursue your passion alone. This child became your affirmation many times.

I sat there dumbfounded, it was true and I remember saying those things. You know that old saying 'be careful what you wish for'. **Universal Law** (ask and you shall receive)

I realised then, that I never really believed in those words, (You create your own reality) until that moment. I thought I was a real player in the spiritual arena but I was just bluffing my way, just like so many others.

I kept a low profile regarding my spiritual growth from then on. I was afraid that I would allow myself to get carried away and it was time for me to find balance in my life with my husband and children. The situation had awakened something so profound within me that it took me a long time to realize it. After the incident with my husband I was like a possessed woman, I watched his every move. Like a hawk on its prey. My mind would not let it go. Twenty-four hours a day and then one day I sat and found myself observing my thoughts, suddenly I saw that my mind had me trapped like a caged animal, I was insane. "This has to stop, look at what you are doing to yourself and your husband, you have to let it go or it will kill you" I thought.

I needed to forgive him and myself. Both of us were in pain we mirrored each other's every move. One of us had to let the fear go and to begin to love. To forgive means to give your love as before so I took the first step and returned to love. We had been living our lives through "conditional love". We were living as if it in a competition, except neither of us were winning. The law of attraction was in action, I wanted love and so did he, but someone had to make the first move. Deep down, I believe, we both felt unworthy and we were afraid to accept these feelings. So many couples go through this, looking outside of themselves for love. Always thinking that another person should know your needs, My advise is don't allow this to be you, tell your partner what you need and ask them what they need. Don't take each other for granted. See the good in each other not the lack and do not place conditions around your love. Give freely from "unconditional love" and above all don't ass-u-me. Fear had been a well-known friend in my life but now I know how to give and receive love. Allow forgiveness, faith, gratitude and trust to be a part of your daily prayer.

The biggest lesson for me was the "love of self." When you don't love yourself you don't recognize love when it is there, you think people have an ulterior motive. I did the work on myself, knowing that if I loved who I was then I could accept that others could love me as well. I began to see my husband in a new light. I no longer focused on what he wasn't doing right and praised him more. This was a doorway into love at a much deeper level and I was grateful that my soul had awakened this part of me to see a bigger picture. My husband and I fulfilled our initial contract and we were now ready for a new love affair to begin.

THE ROAD AHEAD

I was again ready for a new challenge in my life. I was not sure if I was ready to return to massage while housemaid work I found boring. The idea of owning a motel was in the back of my mind and I told my husband of my great idea. "Where would we get the money for that?" he asked. "Why the bank of course" I replied. I put my trust in the universe and felt that this would be our next challenge.

On our daily morning walk my husband and I walked past a local real estate office. In the Office window was a sign to buy a motel lease in town for $250,000. "There it is that's the sign" I said. "We can buy this lease". My husband in his usual 'here she goes again tone' said "there is no way the bank will lend us that amount of money". "How do you know?" I asked. "It is not a lot of money these days compared to the price of houses, you will never know if you don't ask" I added. Once I get an idea in my head, I am like a dog with a bone. My poor husband knew he was in for an ear bashing, so he agreed to see the real estate to get some details. The excitement was building, everything about the motel sounded great. We looked at other motels to compare prices. Now all we had to do was make an appointment with the bank. I posted affirmations all over the house. I visualised every day the perfect outcome and believed if it was to be Gods plan for us, it would happen.

I was very nervous going into the bank with my husband. The bank manager examined the Motel's paper work carefully and finally he looked up and said "as far as I am concerned it all looks very positive. All I ask you to do is to go and discuss it with your accountant and get his opinion first. Then come back to me if all goes well and we will draw up a proposal".

I could have been knocked me over with a feather. We both walked out of the bank a little shell shocked. The universe was saying "YES". Our next step was to consult our accountant. He looked over all the paperwork, as well as the terms from the bank. "Go for it" he said "I think it is a great idea. It will be a great super fund for you in the future". We set off to the real estate to make an offer and the motel owners accepted.

On February the 8th 2004 we took over the lease to the motel. We were scared as hell but I figured I had been to hell and back a few times now and I was starting to get the hang of it. The acronym for fear is: feel excited and ready. I was ready for the next challenge. Our family and friends were in awe of us. They said that it was something they would have liked to do but they lacked the confidence.

My husband decided to keep his job at the mines for a while. He was on a four day on, four day off roster and the extra money came in handy. We worked really well as a team. Our two daughters became part of the team, helping us out whenever they could. The first month was the hardest, getting into a routine, but I loved it all the same. I felt alive again serving the customers with good old fashioned hospitality. A few months passed and problems began to arise. First the hot water system and then the phone system broke down costing us thousands of dollars. I felt like my plans were falling apart.

Tension began building between my husband and me. The stress was again taking a toll on our relationship. I felt my husband was beginning to resent the motel and that he felt pressured into buying it. He also seemed to have doubts about our relationship. "Please don't do this again" I said. "We have made a commitment to this motel and a commitment to us". I was running on autopilot. I found it hard putting on a happy face in front of the customers when all I wanted to do was cry. "I can't do this" I said to my husband. "You have to make up your mind, stay or go". After this confrontation we tiptoed around each other for months. I believe he felt imprisoned and in a way he was right. The motel and his job at the mine kept him so busy he had no free time and in a strange way that made me feel safe. My health was beginning to take a beating. I was plagued with stomach pain and a trip to the specialist confirmed that I had endometriosis. A section of my bowel needed to be removed immediately. The doctor scheduled the operation for September and my parents agreed to come to help our daughters run the motel. I was to be in hospital for seven days and then not allowed to do anything for four weeks. My husband took time off work to be with me. He was wonderful company at the hospital. My knight in shining armour was back. Seeing me lying in the hospital bed after the operation, I could see he was worried.

I believe that at times you only find out how much you love someone when you think you may lose them. I believe this happened to my husband as he went out and bought me the most beautiful eternity ring. "My love for you will last an eternity" he told me. "This is the moment I had been waiting for" I said as I cried tears of joy. When we arrived home everyone knew that something was different between us.

My parents and our daughters had done a wonderful job taking care of the motel. We were grateful that they had come to help us and I believe it made them feel good too. They not only felt needed but saw themselves as capable and effective people. When I felt strong enough my parents went home for a long earned rest. The motel was becoming busier everyday our main clientele were contractors who worked at the mines. We not only did the breakfast and evening meals but we also made lunches for the men on shiftwork. It was very busy, especially in the evenings when all the workmen came in and ordered dinner.

My husband attempted to exercise when he could and I encouraged him to do this for his own sanity. One morning he went out for his usual run when soon afterwards I received a call from the local caravan park. The woman on the phone said my husband was sitting on the footpath outside the park and could I come straight away and to pick him up. I left my two daughters in charge while I went to get him. When I arrived he looked grey and I asked him what was wrong and he told me he felt clammy, out of breath and nauseous. He said "I just need to go home and sit in front of the air conditioner". I took him straight to the doctor's surgery. When we arrived they put him on the ECG machine. "We need to get you to the hospital now" the doctor said and he rang for an ambulance. "We think you are having a heart attack". "No way" my husband said "I don't feel that sick". At the hospital tests confirmed the heart attack. Although experiencing some pain and pin and needles he still couldn't understand. "I can't be having a heart attack, don't you have to be in a lot of pain?" he asked. He was then flown to a hospital in Brisbane with the Royal Flying Doctor Service.

I returned to the motel and once again rang my parents to see if they could help. My husband's parents and his sister all agreed to drive from New South Wales to the hospital the next day. I arrived at the hospital that night to find him in intensive care with machines monitoring his every move. He was sitting in bed and he said "I don't know what all the fuss is about I don't feel like I'm having a heart attack. The doctors say I have two blocked arteries and I am going down for surgery tomorrow morning". I wanted to be strong for him but I thought this time I could really lose him. The nurses were wonderful they sat down and explained to us in detail what was happening to him and what was to happen during the operation.. I explained that his family would arrive in the morning so he could see them before he was to go in for surgery. "Why is everyone making a big fuss over me? They didn't have to come all this way" he said. "No they didn't but they wanted to because you are their only son and they love you" I replied. He smiled and deep down I knew he was happy he just wished it was under better circumstances.

The next morning as he was waiting to go to the operating theatre I could not hold back the emotion I felt.I burst into tears.

"What's all that for?" he asked. "I can't help it. It's the thought of losing you. Please come back to me" I said. He stared into my eyes for what seemed to be an eternity and rested his hand on my cheek and he said "Don't worry I will be coming back." After what seemed like the longest two hours he was back in intensive care room. There was definitely a change in him. He seemed much more loving towards me. His family and I rented a unit near the hospital and after a few days he was allowed to move into the unit with us and a week later he was allowed to go home. He was very weak and even walking exhausted him. We would go down to the river for daily exercise and rest when needed. One day when we were alone he said "You know when you were crying at the hospital before I went to surgery?" "Yes" I said. "Well, when I looked into your eyes I saw exactly how much you loved me. I guess a part of me didn't believe you could love me after the hurt I had put you through". His heart attack was the catalyst for healing his broken heart. And that is what I tell people today that his heart attack was a blessing in disguise.

I realised living in a relationship you can get caught up with the ego and self delusion which constantly challenges your fears of anger, judgement, self-worth and resentment. Woman I believe are particularly challenged by thoughts such as why an unresponsive man doesn't understand her. This then triggers past emotional pain. Thoughts such as "I'm not pretty enough. I'm too fat. I'm too thin are the reasoning into "that's why he doesn't show me any affection". Women then may attack, blame, criticize and even blame the male for all perceived hurts. Both people may then begin to attack and counterattacks. Both have had their 'buttons pushed' and without communicating honestly their thoughts, doubts and fears. The anger simmers never reaching boiling point because the lid is left on only letting out a bit of the steam every now and then. Life proceeds as 'normal' until the next episode. The wheel of life keeps turning and I believe people rarely take the time to stop the wheel to take time to reflect on the events in their lives and why they get upset. You need to become conscious of your triggers and really see them for what they are. You need to become a watcher and to catch your ego out. Learn to press the pause button, stop and take a good look in the mirror. Allow the feelings to surface so you can feel and see your thoughts and feelings for what they really are. See the pain that you have held onto from the past pain that no longer serves you. Learn to stay focused in the now and become a witness to your thoughts. When you do new doors will begin to open in your life and with your relationships. Whenever anything happened to me in I would question "Why god?" and all he ever said was 'KNOW THY SELF'. Remember as you walk your Soul's Way and you feel the urge to change another person, don't let the ego trick you. You can only change yourself and change your perceptions of the world and the people around you. The people around you cannot help but change with you. They will no longer follow you but they will walk beside you.

After my husband and I had lived through the dark night of the soul we found a new level of trust and openness in our relationship. Now we had a second chance at our life together. Our fears no longer ruled us, our hearts took over.

We poured everything we had into the motel and even though it was old and things were breaking down, we learned so much about ourselves. The motel and our experiences showed us that anybody, no matter what their background, can achieve their heart's desire. I now strongly believe: Be clear with your intentions. Be still long enough to hear the answers. And most of all, don't forget to ask your Angels and Guides for help when you need it as you do not need to do it alone.

Three years later and we decided it was time to sell the motel. We did not have many years left on the lease could have made it difficult to sell. I had the idea of writing to the owner and asking if he would sell us the freehold, that way we could draw up a new lease. After some negotiation, the owner agreed and we went to the bank. Our prayers were answered when the bank and the universe both said yes. We bought the freehold and drew up a new 25-year lease. We had some time to think about where we wanted to go and we both agreed to leave the mining town and to settle on the coast. We sold the lease in September 2006 and we jumped in the car and headed off to our new life.

My husband decided to give up the mining game after 21years and took a long earned rest before looking for a new job. It was so nice to sleep in and not have to get up and cook a dozen breakfasts. Having time to spend together for the first time in years we thoroughly enjoyed it!

While out shopping one day I ran into a former massage teacher of mine, Yvonne, and she asked me if I was looking for work. "Not at the moment" I said. "We are having a rest before we go looking". "I know where you can get work massaging again if you are interested" she said. "I work a couple of days at a beauty salon and they need another therapist". I had not thought about going back to massage but after discussing it with my husband I thought I could give it a go. I rang the woman in charge and within two weeks I had a job. I was very nervous and the old thought patterns began to creep back in. "What if nobody likes me?" "What if I am not very good at this?" "Ok that's it Marianne. When are you going to get over yourself, you're still carting around the same old baggage!" I had thought I was over all my insecurities but it showed me the many layers there are to such feelings and thoughts.

I liked the salon and the other workers were friendly and I became good friends with Yvonne. I found the massage tiring and most days I would go home exhausted. My husband was not having much luck finding work so he took on a weekend job at a landscaping yard. This eventually led to full time work but it was very exhausting for him, out in the hot sun all day was a whole lot different from working down a black hole for 21 years.

We both were becoming very tired with our jobs and knew that it was time to look for something else. My husband saw an ad for a job back in the mines working seven days on and seven days off. "Do you really want to go back there?" I asked. "Well I don't see I have much choice at the moment as there is no work in town for me". He applied and got the job and it meant three hours travel to the mine and back. I missed him terribly but it was a bonus when he came home for seven days. We soon adjusted and he felt as if he was semi retired. It was the first time I had seen him happy in years and others also saw the change in him. I decided to resign from my job. My body was in a lot of pain and it was I felt time to start to listen to its messages. It's funny for I now believe your soul will push you into situations where you have to either stop, look, listen and learn or you will find issues repeating themselves until you deal with them in a constructive, thoughtful manner. I really did believe at one stage that by keeping busy all my problems would just go away.

I began to meditate again. It had always had a positive impact on me. I needed to start trusting myself again and to allow my Soul to show me the way.

Our first Christmas on the coast was one of disappointment because I had hoped that our two older children would come to visit for the holidays with the grandchildren. As a mother I was still having control issues. The ones "mother knows best" and as my wise husband explains it you have to cut the cords of attachment. Do I listen NO…. instead I torture myself into believing that I am responsible for making everyone happy. This lesson was one of my biggest. To learn detachment was hard for me. I would continually ring my daughter asking when she was coming to visit. I even suggested that I would travel to pick her up and the children. Each time however she would change the subject. Finally the 'light bulb' switched on. I was trying to control her life instead of allowing her to make choices for herself.

My body had been sending me signals for years. Signals that were trying to tell me not to live my life through everyone else but to live the life that I wanted to live. A new day had dawned. My children showed me how to "let go" and how to allow them to make their own choices. This I did by encouraging them to listen to their own inner guidance and then by assisting them to trust their decisions. I believe this helped them to develop into unique individuals. Of course my husband and I always provide support when needed.

For years I ignored the pain in my body. I had controlled it with pain killers that often kept me dazed and confused. Then one day I made the decision to wake up and to smell the roses by blessing each day.

While my husband and I took some time out for some R & R on the Sunshine Coast, we were awoken by my mobile phone ringing. It was my brother ringing to tell me that our father had been taken to hospital after suffering a bad fall. Within the hour we were travelling to New South Wales. We drove all day and arrived at the hospital around 8.30pm. I was shocked when I saw my father. His face looked like he had gone ten rounds with Mike Tyson. My parents had been visiting my brother when dad went to get the suitcases out of the car. He suffered a dizzy spell and fell down my brother's steep driveway. His face planted on the road and he had severe bruising and bleeding to the brain. He had two black eyes, lacerations all over his face, a broken nose and a whopping big headache. I had only recently returned from visiting my parents in Brisbane as my mother had been to see a specialist. As I was standing beside my father's hospital bed I remembered the words my mother had said to me during the visit in Brisbane. (I wish we had more time to spend with you) and (I don't know what I would do if anything happened to your father). "Wow" This is powerful stuff. The universe is really showing me the power of our thoughts and the energy behind the spoken word.

My husband and I drove back home to Queensland after a couple of days as he had work commitments. My father stayed in hospital for ten days and needed homecare and as my mother was not well enough to take care of him I arranged a three week visit to ensure dad got back on his feet. It was so different. I felt like the parent and that they were my children. We had quality time together. In my spare time I read the book *"The Power of Intention"* by Wayne Dyer and never before had I felt so determined and enlightened after reading a book. Every morning as I went for my walk to clear my head I would talk to God and give thanks for everyone and everything in my life. I had a wonderful dialogue going with myself saying affirmations and the more I said them the more power I felt behind the words. I really believed for the first time what I was saying. Often in the past I would recite affirmations but the belief wasn't always there. The saying "fake it until you make it" well I finally made it! With each passing day, I could feel the words of gratitude touch my soul and tears of absolute joy would run down my face, every cell was tingling with excitement. My eyes were opened with a new perception of who I was. In the past, I struggled with my image, but now I had a new appreciation of ME! I really loved me!

My new understanding opened the doors of forgiveness and I could see the divine plan of my life unfold. I saw everyone and everything that had participated in my life, for who and what they really were, joined together as one mind, acting out the creative dance of my life and theirs. I understood the role we played in each other's lives and in that moment my heart was filled with grace.

Don't ever give up on yourself, for love and joy is available to everyone. Believe and joy will find you. You, Me, Mine are what we identify with. Thoughts of I am fat, I'm not smart enough, I am broke, nobody loves me, I am stupid, I am sick. These thought's will keep you stuck until you really begin to question your thoughts and your ego, where did all these thoughts come from? You will always receive an answer. Only through struggle do we find success, how else do we learn the difference. Be the change yourself and do not expect all good things to come from outside you.

"Be the Change you hope to see in the world" *Muhandas Gandhi*

That's what the ego can stand for, Everything Good Outside. The ego is like an alien in a hostile world where it believes everyone is your enemy, it feeds on drama, it will seek it out like an animal, and we need to control the animal instinct inside of us. We identify with all the drama and when it finally ends we feel somewhat sad and at a loss. This is because drama is all we knew and it feeds our egos and keeps us in our comfort zone .

When I arrived home my family had a new appreciation of me. Absence really does make the heart grow fonder. My daughter was expecting her fourth child which meant she had three children under the age of three and an eight year old! I could see a lot of me in my daughter and that she had chosen a difficult path in life. After the birth my husband and I drove down to see our new grandson. I felt she needed help as she lived in an isolated area but was too proud to ask. As her mother I was afraid for her health and sanity but I admired her for her strength and determination. We did what we could to help her with the children in the little time we had. We went shopping and ensured she had enough food and nappies. We spoke with the local nurse to see if she was able to arrange some home care for her. When the time came to leave it was heartbreaking for us. I cried most of the way home on our seven-hour trip. We barely spoke on the return journey as feelings of guilt arose about leaving her alone. The next day after arriving home, I became very ill with a virus and I knew that I had absorbed all the fear that surrounded my leaving her to cope on her own. I had allowed myself to get caught up in her story and I knew the best thing for me to do was to surround her and the children with love. I also had faith in God's plan for them. I admired her for the role that she has chose to play, seeing firsthand the strength and courage of the human spirit and what it is willing to endure. Watching her movie unfold I was taught the wonderful lesson of detachment and compassion.

Movie star

All I ever wanted was to be heard,
Why does that seem so absurd?
I needed love and understanding,
That is what I wanted to say,
To speak the truth, otherwise fade away.
The road sometimes seems long
That I needed to travel,
However, at the end, there is a mystery to unravel.

JOIN THE HAY MOVEMENT

Looking for inspiration one day I went to the local shopping centre. Upon walking into the local newsagency I felt the need to buy a magazine called *Insight*. It was a magazine I had often brought when I owned the health food store because it was always full of inspiring stories and articles. The main story in the issue I felt compelled to buy was a featured article about Louise Hay. The article explained that she had released a movie, based on her book "*You Can Heal Your Life*". "That's it" I thought. "I need to watch that movie". I then drove into the city and went to a new age store that I hoped would have it. Sure enough, there it was on the shelf. Thankyou universe I thought. I couldn't wait to get home to watch it. I absolutely loved the movie. Something inside me reawakened. Next I came across an ad for a Louise Hay Teacher training course. I got goose bumps and a voice inside me said "you have to look at this". I remembered clearly the Louise Hay workshop I had attended fourteen years previously. I also recalled my thought that one day I would teach this workshop. 'Wow'! I thought "another self fulfilling prophecy". I was super excited. I looked up the details of the course and immediately sent an email to the teacher asking for an enrolment form. It was to be in Victoria, the 20th of September. My first thoughts were about the distance and how far I would have to travel on my own. I was unsure if I could do it. Fear had again risen but as Susan Jeffers says in the title of her book (*Feel The Fear And Do It Anyway)*. I struggled with my ego and fear for days until I finally plucked up the courage to ring the teacher, Susie Mulholland. After talking to Susie, I knew it was the right thing for me to do. So I said YES!

Having discussed my plan with my very supportive husband he soon sourced my plane tickets. I was so excited. I wanted to shout it out to the whole world. I had never been this excited about a course before. The next day I went to the bank and transferred my deposit. That is when it really hit home to me. "This is really happening, I am going to be a certified workshop leader teaching the philosophy of Louise Hay" I proudly thought. I felt I had come full circle with Louise Hay's book *'The Power Is within You"* being a catalyst for my spiritual Journey. I truly feel like one of Louise's success stories. I was about to embrace the best decade of my life so far.

The months leading up to the course I was faced with more lessons regarding one of my children. I discovered my credit card details had been taken and one of my children had been using it to pay off their debts. I was unaware until my account came in the mail. I was devastated to find they had racked up over three thousand dollars worth of debt. I was angry and hurt, even to the point where I thought about ringing the police. I felt so sick in my stomach. I went and sat on my bed and sobbed for hours, until the pain and anger was gone. I sat up and took some deep breaths and I calmed myself. I asked myself "What would Louise Hay or Jesus do in this situation?" these words came "forgive them for they know not what they do". I immediately felt a light surround me and in that moment I was filled with compassion. I was able to stand in their shoes and to feel their fear and pain. I rang the next day to tell them that they were forgiven even though we did not condone what they had done we still loved them very much. I also explained that the same love flows within them. I did a meditation that same day where I saw them living a happy and fulfilled life. I then cut the cords and released everything to God. This lesson had been showing up in my life in little ways, but I wasn't fully ready to let go of the drama. My Soul always knew however when the time was right. Controlling the anger first, stepping aside and asking for a better solution was a major step for me.

By September I had worked for months with affirmations and visualisations of the Hay Teacher training course all of these boosted my confidence and trust in life. Arriving at Albury Airport on Saturday 20th September Susie's partner Pete collected all the course participants in a bus. I introduced myself to the other women and enjoyed the beautiful scenery on the forty-minute drive to the resort. The course was held at La Trobe Resort, which was once the Lunatic asylum or as I preferred to call it the May Day Hills Hospital. It had been built in 1867 as one of three Asylums in Victoria. The resort overlooked the beautiful town of Beechworth, the grounds were stunning. The Latrobe University acquired the property in 1996 and has systematically restored and renovated the site. The rooms for participants were in the old nurse's quarters. Huge metal doors that once closed off each section could be seen throughout the complex.

I had time on the Saturday to walk to town to view the wonderful history of Beechworth. The town dates back to the boom days of the goldfields. Today it contains historic hotels, cafes, antique shops and art galleries. I spent the afternoon window shopping and taking in the beautiful scenery. Registration for the workshop was at 5.00pm that night. I was anxious but eager to meet everyone. I also met the other women who were my roommates for the week. They were all friendly and that me reassurance me.

At the commencement of the course we had to introduce ourselves and I felt ok until it was my turn. My heart was trying to jump out my throat, and tears were beginning to well up in my eyes. "NO! Hold it together Marianne. Get a grip. You can do this" I thought. I didn't want to fall into an emotional mess on the first night, so I quickly blurted out why I thought I was there and passed it over to the next person. It turned out to be a fun night. We all bonded as if it was a huge family reunion. For the first two days we participated in the *Heal Your Life Workshop* "piece of cake" I thought. I had previously completed the workshop twice but little did I realize the amazing healing power of such a large group. Nothing like peeling away more layers of the past and putting all of your issues in the tissues with lots of group hugs. The group dynamics after those first two days was amazing. I had never experienced sisterhood like this before. It was truly something special to behold and to take part in.

I remembered Louise Hay's words from her book **You Can Heal Your Life** about planting your seeds and watching them grow. When I arrived at the course I felt like a tiny little seed amongst a big group of seeds, trying to find my fertile patch of soil. I wasn't quite sure where to plant my seed.

One afternoon during the course we were to choose a place outside. The criteria was "select any place you feel drawn to, sit for a while in the stillness and ask yourself what it is you need to heal and then allow the answer to come from nature itself". I felt drawn to a beautiful majestic gum tree and I turned around and leaned back against the trunk. The word 'FEAR' kept flashing in my mind and then a stream of words began to form in my mind. It didn't feel as if the words belonged to me. Then I realized the tree was talking to me I reached for my journal and started to write the words to the following poem.

Fear

'FEAR' There is nothing to fear but fear itself,
Look at me for here I am, standing tall
Look at my body there are many scars,
I have seen many seasons and yet I am still
standing,
No matter what Mother Nature has thrown at me,
I have never stopped growing.
I have many branches that lead to nowhere,
Yet my centre still grows toward the light.
I am majestic I am strong,
Many a bird has rested their weary wings,
Until it becomes safe for them to fly.
We are the same you and I,
Allow your seeds to spread far and wide,
Mother earth will rejoice in the birth of her
children.

Afterwards we assembled together and there was a calm silence in the room. I felt a surge of energy as if it was urgent for me to speak up and to share my experience. I did not want to go first however so I waited. I spoke to the group next and as I started to speak I felt as if I was part of that gum tree. I read my poem with tears streaming down my face and when I looked up at the group they were all crying with me. I was so overwhelmed with emotion I had to leave the room. I felt as if Mother Nature had welcomed me back home and it felt wonderful.

As a child I loved being out in nature and I would collect all sorts of things leaves, rocks, flowers, lizards and beetles. I would then give them a home under my bed, much to my mother's horror! I believe that as adults we tend to lose our connection with mother earth, and I was grateful to have this chance to reconnect in the most divine way.

Everybody in the group shared their heartfelt stories with Mother Earth and her family. It seemed like divine timing and we were ready for a new chapter in our lives with the universe supporting us in every way. Our last day together was inspiring. We shared a beautiful bond of giving and receiving. It will last in my heart and memory forever. I took my seed home, to plant in the rich soil. I nurtured it, nourished it and gave it all the love it required for it to realize its full potential.

On my trip home my flight from Sydney to Brisbane was delayed this meant I was to miss my last connection home. I wasn't angry just disappointed that I wouldn't be seeing my family that night. The airline arranged for the passengers to spend the evening in Brisbane. All expenses paid including taxi fares, an evening meal, a beautiful room at the Seibel and a full breakfast. I felt a gift from the universe was given to me as a reward for the past week. I accepted it and said "Thank you, Thank you, and Thank you".

When I arrived home the next day, I was exhausted but I had to start back at work. I worked as a demonstration cook for a local chicken shop. The job had provided me with the money for the workshop. The job also helped to build my confidence. It required that I stand at the front of the shop to talk to people. This prepared me for the future.

I knew preparing for the *Heal Your Life Workshops* would be costly and would take preparation, so I stayed as the cook for a few more months to help pay for the setup costs. I had a lot of work to do designing flyers on the computer and setting dates for my first workshop. I went to new age stores, libraries, bookshops and massage clinics and asked if they would display my flyers. Within a week I received phone calls and most people were very keen to start right away. I explained as Christmas was approaching I wasn't holding a workshop until the New Year. I then contacted them and scheduled my first workshop for February the 7th and 8th.2009. I managed to find a hall that was suitable in a quiet street away from any noise.

With my renewed faith, I said a prayer to my angels for them to bring the perfect group together. I put an additional advert in the local paper and trusted that the right people would see it. I was saying daily affirmations such as:

"My body has restored itself to its natural state of health"
"I love and accept myself exactly as I am"
"I am a powerful healer and intuitive"
"I am happy and at peace with myself"
"All is well in my world"

All did feel well in my world, until I began to get a searing pain in my left leg. Initially I thought I had pulled a hamstring while attending a yoga class. I rang my friend Yvonne for a massage and as luck had it she just got a cancellation. Once she started massaging my hamstring wasn't sore and she told me that it was more likely to be sciatica. "I've never felt sciatica this bad before" I said. I hoped I hadn't stirred up an old injury. On the way home I had a terrible urgency to go the toilet and I stopped at the supermarket. I rushed to the toilets and it felt like my bladder wasn't able to empty properly. I then hurried home. By now my leg was burning and my tummy was bloated and irritable. I raced back to the toilet only this time I could not leave. My urinary tract had gone into a complete spasm and urine was trickling out constantly. I rang my doctor to get some advice and he told me to go to the hospital. By the time I reached the hospital I was in agony I couldn't keep off the toilet. The nurse gave me a tablet and then sent me home. When I arrived home it was worse. I sat on the toilet for an hour, not able to move, so I again rang my doctor. He suggested I ring for an ambulance as he was concerned that I may be suffering not from an infection but from a spinal injury. As the ambulance was sent for I became completely overcome with fear. I began to play terrible scenarios over in my mind. I found my new affirmations were uncovering other layer of fears and bringing them up to the surface. These needed healing. The memory of my damaged discs from1990 came flooding back. My doctor at the time had told me that in the future it may mean I could lose control of my bladder and bowel. This was because of the damage in relation to the nerves in my spine. I remember going home to my husband petrified, feeling angry and pissed off with the doctor, regarding his prognosis. "How dare he tell me that" I yelled. So there it was all the emotion behind the cause. I had held on to this fear since then but now I was ready to release the anger and fear. I also needed to forgive the doctor. This healing prepared me for what was beginning to unfold in my mind. Two words, "Control Freak"! recognizing the emotions behind the cause helped me to forgive and let go, within a couple of days I was feeling better as well as taking the antibiotics.

Leading up to the first workshop I was slipping back into the old controlling mode of worrying about why the phone wasn't ringing? Was I going to get enough people? Would I cover all my expenses? There they were those old familiar thought patterns. At least now though I was able to catch them out by remaining aware and then by releasing them to God.

The following day the phone began to ring and I was well on my way to holding my first workshop. I had asked the Angels to bring the perfect group together and they never let me down. I started my workshop with four lovely women and although very nervous, the weekend turned out perfectly. I however did not realize just how much emotional energy it took to run the workshop. I went home and crashed on the lounge and fell asleep.

FROM LITTLE THINGS BIG THINGS GROW

My first workshop and I broke even financially. My faith in my daily prosperity affirmations were starting to manifest. I would say "money flows into my life, from all expected and unexpected sources". Not long after my two eldest children decided to pay back the money they had borrowed. I smiled at my husband and said "how about that for unexpected resources". We both had believed we would never see that money again (sorry kids) it wasn't a small amount it was a few thousand dollars. Then my old boss rang about me returning to work. I believe this was a lesson for me to be very specific when saying your affirmations. Be careful what you wish for.

I then had a conversation with a client regarding healing affirmations. She explained that after saying her affirmations religiously for about a week or two she started to feel sick and withdrawn. I could relate that to my own experience when I had the sciatic pain. My body was bringing to the surface emotions ready to be released. These took the form of pain and illness. I believe it is just like going on a health kick. After a couple of days your body begins to detoxify. Affirmations not only re-program your mind but also your body. It is I believe only natural that your body will want to be rid of any old stored conditioned patterns. Be gentle with yourself and allow your body to heal and this feeling should pass. Do things such as a long soak in a bath or go for a walk in nature but don't fall back into the old habit of thinking that the affirmations are not working because they definitely are.

Look in the mirror and ask yourself what is it that your inner child would like to do today. Have fun with it. Do not let your ego get the upper hand and rain on your parade. You will discover that loving and accepting yourself will get easier when you learn not to be so hard on yourself. It is a common misconception that what we react too much. Is it something or someone outside of us? The ego would have us believe that it is. It would have us believe that our partners or friends push our buttons that it's their fault. "So and so made me late". "I can't do what I really want to do because my partner won't approve". Sound familiar? When the penny finally drops and we realize it is our own thoughts that are making us crazy, it is so liberating. Stand back, become the observer, for everyone who crosses your path is your teacher, mirroring back to you your beliefs and judgements. When you can align your thoughts with God, which means thinking from your heart and not your head you are well on your way to universal unconditional love.

UNI VERSE can be interpreted as united (in) verse. This then can mean we become one with our thoughts and actions and realize that we are all connected as God's children.

HOME SWEET HOME ·

 have always wanted to work from home but I was having
trouble finding suitable venues that were affordable for my
workshops. It was time for a new set of affirmations. I wrote down
all the things I wanted in a new home. It had to have at least
four bedrooms, two bathrooms, a large extra room to hold my
workshops and landscaped gardens for people to enjoy the beauty
of nature. I wanted also to create a wonderful healing space and of
course it had to be at an affordable price.

Each morning on my daily walk I would visualize and recite my
affirmations. Next I would hand them over to the angels. I did this
every day for two months and one morning while I was meditating,
I received a message to go and look at an open house down the
street where I lived. I grabbed my daughter, as my husband was
away at work, and we walked down the street to where the open
house was. The agent was greeting everyone at the door; I did know
the owner briefly as I had worked with her son. At the front of the
house had been converted into a large playroom as the owner had
run her own child care centre from home. The home was bigger
than I expected with five bedrooms, two bathrooms and a study.

It was set on an acre of land with landscaped gardens and views of the local mountains. It was everything I had been asking for and more. I was so excited I rang my husband to tell him the news. He agreed to view the house on the computer. The next day he rang me and explained the house was under contract as someone had already put an offer in. I told him not to worry as I had a feeling that the people wouldn't be able to get the finance. He gave a little laugh and said "Ok darling we will see what happens when I get home in a couple of days". The next day I rang the Real Estate agent to ask about the house and she explained that she had just got off the phone to the people who had made an offer and they were unable to get finance!. Of course, you couldn't wipe the smile off my face. In the meantime my friend Janelle viewed the house while visiting me. I was so excited when telling her about the house and I was keen to get her ideas about the house. Janelle liked it but wasn't taken with it as I was. She asked if I had looked at other homes in the area. I had been looking for a while, but nothing suited like this one. I started to have second thoughts; maybe she is right there might be something better. Janelle went home the next day and I was feeling a bit down when it hit me like a lightning bolt. I never listen to myself. I always think that other people know better. I silently sent a thank you to my friend for showing me my dilemma. I loved the house and the universe agreed with me. My husband was due home the next day. I thought if he loves the house like I do then it was meant for us, if he doesn't like it then I know God has another plan. I arranged with the agent to have another house inspection. My husband and I took our time and inspected the entire house. My husband had his poker face so I couldn't judge his thoughts. I couldn't wait to get home to ask him what he thought. "Well what do you think? Do you like it?". "I love it" he said "Now let's ring the agent and make an offer". It was on the market for $629,000 and we had never dreamed of being able to afford such a house. As luck would have it two months prior we had been able to sell the freehold of the motel. So we were now able to afford the house. The angels had told me that we would get the house for $600,000. So when we put in our bid and the owners agreed on that exact price. I just love it when a plan comes together. I was grateful to the universe for providing us with opportunity to purchase our dream home.

I was on cloud nine, complete happiness overwhelmed me. "It works! It really works"!

I kept saying to my husband. "You can't deny the proof". In the following weeks I scheduled more workshops from my new home. My mantra at the time was: Live and Let God. I now believe my controlling streak disrupted my first attempt at holding a workshop. I knew I had to slow down and tune into my breath. Understanding what the mystics say, go with the flow or 'the breath of life' brings about a sense of peace. Stay with the breath and you will find the way.

We are, I believe, born into this world when we take our first breath. I remember what it is like to watch a new baby breathe. Our 'breath' brings us into being and we listen to our Soul breathing the universal language of peace and harmony. I now find myself seeking more solitude. I turn off the TV and radio. I am now happy and content listening to my breath and the world around me. To me it is like living in a parallel universe and now I

understand the term 'veils of illusion'. These moments are not always there mind you but they are becoming more frequent in my life. I choose every day for my higher self to rule my mind and body, to choose the eyes of God and not the eyes of the ego.

My husband and I created a sacred space in our new garden for people to feel safe and at peace. Once this was done I was now ready to hold another workshop. God delivered to my door a wonderful group of eight women. This group was a perfect group. This group loved my home and the created space. Everyone felt safe. On the second day of the workshop two women experienced healings and they left that day looking and feeling completely different. I knew then that this was the right place. I felt ecstatic. I remember reading Louise Hays account about her first time on the podium as a public speaker. How as she finished her first appearance she walked away saying to **herself "Louise you were wonderful. You were absolutely fantastic for the first time. When you have done five or six of these, you will be a pro".** (*You Can Heal Your Life chapter nine.)* She refused to criticize herself in any way. By her sixth time she was feeling like a pro.

I would not have changed anything about that weekend. I was so proud of myself. I now knew that I was a confident inspiring teacher just as I had been affirming. I had come to trust myself fully, knowing divine order knows best. To be able to share in the transformation of these wonderful women and to witness the miracles that took place was awe-inspiring and MAGICAL!

As the days followed my world definitely changed. Firstly an email came asking me if I was a spiritual counsellor/healer. I was unsure how to respond to it. I felt like I was in a vortex with the day of reckoning having arrived. My tiny seed had grown into a tree and it was beginning to branch out. As my husband was waiting to reply to the email I looked him the eye and said "YES I AM". I felt as if I was taking an oath, the truth and nothing but the truth. I accepted regardless of the trembling fear I felt. A fear I knew too well. I was ready to live my life in alignment with my highest purpose. I believed the truth had now set me free. Within a couple of days I received another email asking me the same thing. It showed me that the universe has a sense of humour and that maybe this was test to see if I was serious. "Bring it on" I said "I am up for the challenge". My husband, even though he still doesn't fully understand what I do, is very supportive. But that's ok. It's good to have an air of mystery about oneself.

Love

Love is always here,
Allow yourself to feel it, let go of the fear,
Surrender to the universe,
Listen to your heart; listen to your voice,
Because you know, that we always have a choice.
Accept the part you are here to play,
Love will make you stronger day by day,
Relax, as your soul knows the way,
For it is the voice of here, now, today.

MIRACLES ARE EVERYWHERE

My husband works away, seven days on seven days off so we often communicate by phone. During a phone call one day I explained to him about a conversation I had had with a woman that had been to a recent workshop. She had told me how grateful she was that people, such as myself, were doing such important work. She also explained how important she felt it was for other people to understand the ideas from the workshops. She felt that I had explained everything to them so clearly using the KISS technique (keep it simple sweetheart). She was amazed at the transformation within her life that took place that weekend. When I'd finished telling my husband the story he told me that he had goose bumps. I laughed like crazy, that was a miracle in itself. So I thanked the universe for its confirmation of the work I was doing.

I believe I have grown so much since starting this journey. I am grateful for the knowledge and wisdom that God has passed onto these women through me. Being a part of their soul's way to freedom and grace and making a peaceful contribution to the healing of the planet. I grew up thinking that one person could not make a difference to the world. Now I know that "one person" can make a huge difference to the whole. Everyone is a link in the chain and if one person can make another person happy today a ripple effect will be created.

My life has changed so much as I have come into the alignment with the source of all there is. My connection to a mother/ father God has awakened. I now realise my place in the holy trinity is to honour thy father, thy mother and thy self. For many years I thought of God as being disconnected to me. I discovered that I was the one who was disconnected all along. I was against ritual and prayer, but now I have found it to be a very important tool. Growing up in catholic schools I was always bucking the system not really knowing why I felt that way. Now I know it was all about teaching me to find my own truth.

Remember in order to know oneself *you have to find out who you are not*!

I remember now to greet each day with gratitude and I realise we are living a divine life if we just surrender. We are never alone, our angels, our guides and God are with us 24/7. They lift us up, holding our hand, catching us when we fall, just like when Jesus fell carrying the cross Simon came to help him. He knew his fate just as he also knew that he was loved. He thought his father had abandoned him but he sent him his brother. We don't have to carry the cross alone we have our brothers and sisters.

As I review my life I can see the patterns of abandonment that have played out over the years, each time bringing me closer to who I am. Just like the miracle of finding your own puzzle pieces!

After spending several months on my spiritual growth I realised I had neglected my physical body. One minute you are riding the wave when you realise the tide has gone out and you're stuck there. How did you get there you wonder? I wanted to wake up and embrace the day and the tablets I were on kept me half-asleep. I loved my body but it was high time I treated it with the respect it deserved. My body and I have been through many trials and triumphs so this time I said I can do this again. "I am with you completely" I said, "I will not give up on you".

It was time to face my addiction to pain killers not only for myself but for my family who have kept me strong with their loving support.

Don't dismiss challenges in your life as a step backwards they are lessons to learn that will make you stronger. The minute you label them as wrong you miss the opportunity to love on a deeper level.

A further trial stepped into my life when my eldest daughter was rushed to hospital with stomach cramps. It took three days to discover she had a ruptured spleen. When asked how it happened she explained that her two-year-old son had jumped off the lounge on to her stomach while she was on the floor. Our family had a hard time believing her as her partner had a history of violence. I was told that most cases of ruptured spleen stem from domestic violence. When she was transferred to a larger hospital my husband and I drove eight hours to the hospital. She was separated from her partner and the four young children as they could not get to the hospital to visit. She remained in hospital for two weeks to allow the rupture to heal by itself. She was worried how her partner would cope looking after the children on his own. As a parent you want to jump in and organize their lives because we think we know what's best. We offered to take her four children back home with us so that her partner could return to work. Our minds were very puzzled as we wanted to work out the best possible solution for everyone. I soon realised however that God has a plan. Letting go of the situation and hand it over to God is exactly what I did. I sat back and watched with amazement as the plan unfolded. My daughters' partners' boss gave him two weeks off with pay to take care of the children. He had never before cared for the children on his own, so it provided him time to bond with his family. As for us, it gave us a chance to spend quality time with our daughter and we were able to get to know our daughter all over again. God knew she needed to rest and the children needed their father. It is wonderful when a plan comes together. It becomes a 'divine plan that is'.

BELIEVE IN MIRACLES

Miracles come in all shapes and sizes. I came across a book by Dr John Hinwood and friends called *"You Can Expect a Miracle"*. I was unprepared as to how those three words 'expect a miracle' would impact on my life and the life of others so quickly. In his book Dr Hinwood explained how he made up business cards with the words expect a miracle. He always carried them with him wherever he went. He knew when to give them to people or when to use them for things he wanted. He suggested using them to get a seat on a plane or for a table at a restaurant that was fully booked. In the back of the book he gives the reader sample cards to use and a website to print them out from, www.expectamiracle.com. I printed some of the cards and I then took them to the New Age Gift store where I had begun working. I printed enough cards to put inside the store shopping bags and I would give them out to people whom I believe needed them. A month later an elderly lady came into the shop and told me that after purchasing some crystals she found a little card that said 'expect a miracle'. She explained "I did get my miracle. So I wondered if you had any more of those cards as I have friends who could really do with a miracle". I explained that I would print more and I would leave them at the shop for her next time she came in. A week later another lady came in to tell me about her miracle after receiving a card. She explained that her grown up son had came to visit her bringing his daughter with him. "It's a miracle because I have not seen my son for a few years because of a falling out and I had never met my granddaughter" she said. The cards were weaving their magic in people's lives. Soon afterwards a gentleman came into the store and I gave him a card. He looked at it with a puzzled look on his face at first and then placed it in his wallet. A half an hour later he came back and asked if I had any more cards. He said he had gone to do more shopping and during this time he felt a strong energy emanating from the card. He felt he needed to get more cards so that he could give them out to family and friends. I also gave them out to my friends and family. One of my friends rang me the day afterwards and said "You will never believe what happened to me today." "I was driving home after being at a meeting and I decided to call in at the local club to have a little flutter on the pokies. I walked up to a machine that I had never played before and I won $16,000 dollars. Can you believe it?" she said. "I sure can," I said. How is that for miracles? I think my guides and angels must scratch their heads sometimes wondering how they are ever going to get me to trust their judgements.

Another aspect that entered my life has been giving Angel readings using Doreen Virtues Angel Cards. This I feel is another branch that has grown from my beautiful seed. Amazing messages have come through from spirit and even though I do believe I am always in awe of how the messages come through. For example one day one of the girls working at the shop rang to tell me a lady had booked a reading for the following morning at 9 am. The night before I was awoken at two in the morning and was guided to write down three pages of messages for my client. I easily went back to sleep. Morning came and I was excited to be delivering the messages except the woman did not show up. I tried ringing her number and there was no answer. I packed up and went home thinking to myself she must have become frightened. On my way home however my mobile phone rang it was another lady wanted a reading on that day and she seemed in a great hurry. I asked her to come to my home at one o'clock. I went and sat in my room so I could tune into her energy and I ask the angels for any messages. The response I received was that they had already given me messages. "Wait a minute" I said "They were for the lady at the shop and she didn't show up". "Trust" came the reply. This I did and as it turned out the messages were for my second client. She was amazed and so was I. She told me later that if I could not give her a reading on that day she wasn't sure what she would have done. She said she felt desperate. As it turned out spirit can and does move mountains when they have to. As for the first woman she turned up at the shop at precisely one o'clock thinking that was her appointment time. It clearly wasn't her day. Therefore, as you see trust is a big issue for me. I am getting better though. Another client rang wanting to know if she had really been talking to her mother, who had passed away or if was she just imagining as a means to manage her grief at her loss. I tuned into her mother for her and her mother came through straight away. There was one small problem though she was speaking in Greek. I didn't have a clue as to what she was saying. I then realised I could ask the angels to interpret the message for me. Next I heard the words "talk to her as if it is a picture". I was also told to ask her what her actual name was as well as her birth name. I rang my client to tell her she had definitely been talking and feeling her mum around her. I explained how she came through quickly and that she wanted to tell you "she likes her picture". I asked "Does that mean anything to you?" "Yes" she said. "I took a photo of me and mum before she passed. I had it enlarged and put it in a frame. I keep it beside my bed and I sent copies to my sisters. That is so great" she excitedly said. "I am so glad she likes it". "Well it doesn't stop there" I said. "She also wanted me to ask you what your real name is and your birth name". She was shocked "Get out of here" she replied." I had my name changed by deed poll a few years back because it was hard for people to remember my real name". "Well" I responded she wanted you to know that you really are talking to her and to stop doubting. "I know I won't" she replied.

I had just completed running my eighth *Heal Your Life Workshop* and I have grown in confidence. Sometimes though the lessons I have learnt I feel are greater for me than those of the participants. The eighth workshop was a good blend of energies with an amazing group of women. By the end of day one however I was unsure if one of the ladies would be return the next day. She had grown very agitated with the exercises and she found the writing activities difficult. The Inner-child exercise had obviously stirred up anger issues and she was having trouble understanding what was going on. The logical mind didn't want her to know and was blocking her intuitive knowing. I sat and explained to her about the ego and the battle it can put you through to stop you from growing. I explained that even though I couldn't make her do the exercises I was asking her to go inside her heart to see if she was willing to give it a try. "You have come this far already" I said. "Now ask yourself do you want to go forward or back?" At the end of the first day everyone appeared happy, yet exhausted. To my shock the lady about whom I was concerned was the first one to arrive the next morning. She said "I had the weirdest thing happen to me last night". "I was woken around 2.30 a.m by my inner child. She appeared very dark but she was pleading with me to notice her". I then explained that her inner child was letting her know that the workshop was a safe environment for her explore and talk to her child. I also explained it was probably something she had not done for a long time due possibly to painful memories. This woman then appeared at ease and with new determination she began to want to know more about her inner child.

Next came the hug exercise, one of my favourites and I always laugh at the synchronicity as to the partner choosing. There are no mistakes in the universe. While some embraced and got into a comfortable position two women stood like statues. They could not hug each other. They were only able to place their hands on their upper arms and that was as close as they would get. Body language said it all. They were not letting the love in. As we delved further both of these women were in similar relationships and therefore I was not surprised at the dynamics that were playing out. When the music stopped after seven minutes the two women couldn't wait to sit down. The rest of the day was brilliant and for the closing circle I played the song "You're an angel". I asked everyone to sing along and look into each other's eyes to acknowledge what we had shared over the weekend. Not long into the song one of the women from the hug song exercise relaxed and moved across the circle towards the other woman. She embraced her in a huge hug for the rest of the song. Everyone cheered and tears of joy flowed as everyone present witnessed the exchange between these two women. I am sure the women themselves were able to see the angel within each other.

Every workshop is different but I am always amazed at the similarities between the women present at each workshop. The universe does know how to bring groups together. So my advice is whenever in doubt ask the universe to guide you and to bring to you the situations that you are ready to heal. Then sit back and enjoy the ride.

I like to use prayer as it reminds me that I am safe. I believe we can then trust what unfolds and that we are always taken care of. My favourite prayer is the "Serenity Prayer".

"Dear God, give me the serenity to accept the things I cannot change, the courage to change the things I can and the wisdom to know the difference."

I recite my own daily prayer which is:

"Dear father in heaven, thank you for guiding me and taking care of all my needs on this beautiful day.

Dear earth mother, thank you for keeping my family safe and allowing us to live in

Harmony.

I am eternally grateful as your child of the universe. Unite me with your divine consciousness, to serve humanity with loving kindness. AMEN".

EYES WIDE OPEN

I had the pleasure of attending the I CAN DO IT CONFERENCE in Sydney August 2010 run by Hay House. There were five speakers including Wayne Dyer who was making his last trip to Australia. I attended with friends and we all felt the conference for us was a great success. All the speakers had been inspiring and I felt sure that everyone who had attended would return home a different person.

The conference finished on the Sunday and we were feeling excited but sad to leave such a vibrant and energetic environment. As we made our way through the busy shopping centre at Darling Harbour for tea our group stopped at the top of the stairs near the entrance of the food court. It was then that I noticed something at my feet. I picked it up and found it was a silver angel and a cross. I just knew it was a gift from the angels. I then thanked not only the angels but the blessed person who let it go. Why this find was so significant was because prior to the trip I had been thinking about running Angel workshops. But doubt and worry had prevented me from doing this. This I believed was a sign from the Angels to go ahead and to be a messenger and to do what you love. Luckily my eyes were open to see the gift. "Thank you, thank you, thank you" I repeated over and over. I believed who ever had lost the pendant had had a faith in Angels.

The next morning and it was time for us to return home. Waiting outside the motel we realised we had not booked the shuttle bus to the airport. We immediately rang them and the woman answering the phone didn't seem very obliging when she said "You should have booked yesterday. The next shuttle will be at nine fifteen". This was to be too late for us. Even though we had paid for the shuttle in advance we were unable to recoup the money. As we stood on the footpath cursing the shuttle company and wondering what to do I remembered Wayne Dyer's words. "When you change the way you look at things everything changes." I then blessed the shuttle company and asked God for help. Almost straight away a taxi slowly passed by turned around and stoped. "Are you needing a lift to the airport?" asked the taxi driver. One of our group asked "How much will it cost?" "Thirty dollars mam" he said. We all piled into the car. One of the girls who sat in the front seat asked the cab driver where he was from. He explained he had come over from Tibet two years earlier. As he was wearing some unusual beads around his wrist she also asked him about them. "These are prayer beads and they were given to me by the Dalai Lama" he replied. Well we knew in that instant that the Dalai Lama had sent us help in the way of this happy and humble taxi driver. We arrived at the airport in plenty of time and the fare only totalled $23.50. We however gave him the original quoted fare money. No matter how big or small your problem may seem when you change your perception of the situation and allow the universe to work its magic it will!

I say to everyone keep your eyes and hearts open to the gifts that come your way. My life has changed rapidly day by day and I am grateful to people such as Louise Hay for steering me in the direction of my Soul's Way.

"It is not the end it is the beginning".

I have come to the understanding that deep down we all hold a vision of a wonderful place, peace on earth but we often fail to see that it comes from inside of us not outside. It is never lost but it is there in our hearts.

I have always questioned everything in my life. Sometimes I feel a little too much. I don't profess to be anyone special. I don't have a degree. I didn't go to university and as you know I didn't even finish high school but I know I have graduated in the school of life and to me that is all that matters. My thoughts about my life and my beliefs are constantly changing as they have throughout this book.

My Soul is teaching me how to look at things differently and now I look back at my life's journey with love, forgiveness and compassion. Instead of "edging God out" I am again allowing him in. If you have reached a crisis point in your life I recommend you look for a **Heal Your Life Workshop** leader in your area or to log on to www.HayHouse.com. There you will find many inspiring books and events to feed your soul. Be the builder, the creator, and the inventor. Renovate your life. Take that piece of marble that is you and sculpt it into a new form. You are the Master, so Master your destiny, improve it, expand it, and fill it with light. Accept every part of you. Seek the truth amidst all things.

Recently I asked the Angels the following questions.

To define joy.

"Joy is being who you are in every moment."

To define love.

"Love is everything, love is creation, love is allowing, love is being, love is infinite, there is no end to love and no way to define it".

To define karma.

"Karma has been misunderstood just as punishment has been. There is no punishment only experience".

To define illness.

"If you suffer from illness, then you are suffering from not loving, love of self and love of life".

WHERE DO I GO FROM HERE?

I am about to embark on a ten day silent meditation retreat. Another page and chapter is to be added to my Souls journey. I do not know what to expect. I believe my Angels want me to shut up for a while so that they can get through in a clearer manner. As my husband said, with a smile on his face "That (keeping quiet) will probably be my biggest challenge yet". He is probably right! So I say "I'm ready to feel the fear and do it anyway" because now I know that fear stands for Feeling Excited And Ready and not (F**k Everything And Run) which I read in a book called '*Happiness Now'* by Robert Holden. So stay tuned in until next time.

"NAMASTE."

ACKNOWLEDGMENTS

So many years and so many people have helped bring this book to life. My heartfelt thanks goes to all the following people.

Kevin, my wonderful husband and soul mate, whenever I need to remember who I am, you are always there to remind me. Thankyou my darling, you are my anchor.

To my four beautiful children Daniel, Katrina, Kylie and Justin who taught me "to let go". They also showed me ways to follow my own Soul's Way.

To our gorgeous grandchildren, who keep us, "young at heart".

Gratitude and thanks go to my amazing parents, for their love and support, blood, sweat and tears. I believe it was all worth it.

To my brother Stephen, who always stood beside me in my younger years.

Thank you to all my extended family for crossing my path and for keeping the story alive. What a wonderful journey it has been and richer for having you in it.

Thank you to Louise L Hay, Susie Mulholland my "Heal Your Life" teacher and mentor.

And to my many teachers in human form as well as to my Angels and guides, who never gave up on me and I know I was a hard nut to crack.

To the "Heal Your Life" family for continuing to support us all in spreading the word.

Also to all my wonderful friends, too many now to name, but you all know who you are. Keep following your heart's desire.

My heart has grown so much because you have all fulfilled your contract with me.

This book I dedicate to you all and hope you begin to follow your Soul's Way.

To Balboa press and their lovely team for putting this book together and making it a reality.

To Wayne Dyer for sharing his own journey through his inspirational books.